SELFLESS WORTH
Giving life to the value of your relationship

Alexander Young

Copyright © 2020 by **Alexander Young**

All rights reserved. No part of this publication may be reproduced, distributed or transmitted in any form or by any means, including photocopying, recording, or other electronic or mechanical methods, without the prior written permission of the publisher, except in the case of brief quotations embodied in critical reviews and certain other noncommercial uses permitted by copyright law. For permission requests, write to the publisher, addressed "Attention: Permissions Coordinator," at the address below.

Alexander Young/Rejoice Essential Publishing
PO BOX 512
Effingham, SC 29541
www.republishing.org

Unless otherwise indicated, scripture is taken from the King James Version.'

Scriptures taken from the Holy Bible, New International Version®, NIV®. Copyright © 1973, 1978, 1984, 2011 by Biblica, Inc.™ Used by permission of Zondervan. All rights reserved worldwide. www.zondervan.com The "NIV" and "New International Version" are trademarks registered in the United States Patent and Trademark Office by Biblica, Inc.™

Selfless Worth/ Alexander Young

ISBN-13: 978-1-952312-62-5
Library of Congress Control Number: 2021904175

DEDICATION

I dedicate this book to my Lord and Savior, Jesus Christ. He first loved me and gave His life because He values and desires to have a relationship with me as He does with the rest of the world.

TABLE OF CONTENTS

ACKNOWLEDGEMENTS......................................ix

INTRODUCTION..1

CHAPTER 1:   WHERE IS YOUR FOCUS?...........4

CHAPTER 2:   SUPPORT SYSTEM.......................9

CHAPTER 3:   MATTERS OF THE HEART.........15

CHAPTER 4:   CONFLICT RESOLUTION..........26

ABOUT THE AUTHOR..36

ACKNOWLEDGEMENTS

I want to acknowledge My wife, Evelyn Whitfield Young, for being at my side through the good and bad times.

To my Mother, Tanya Algee, thank you for airways pushing, encouraging, and supporting me to achieve my goals.

To my sister and brother, Elder Shona & Michael Dennis, thank you both for always helping me to be an effective speaker.

To Elder Jerry Addy, thank you for always teaching me to have a sense of precision or to pay "attention to detail."

To Bishop Anthony Alfred, you did more than just see potential and value in me. You gave life and value to the leadership within me.

INTRODUCTION

I often asked myself, "Why do couples, married and non-married, break up so easily? Why is the divorce rate is so high?" One day I was at a store and the customer in front of me dropped a penny. I said, "Ma'am, you dropped your penny." She replied, "It's just a penny," as if it has no life or value. I picked up the coin and it dawned on me that many people treat their relationships like this penny. What if I told you that many relationships are failing or have failed because each party is selfish and only concerned with valuing themselves. I am reminded daily how Jesus loves us and values our worth. I'm also reminded of this in a familiar passage of the 'Parable of the lost coin' in Luke 15:8-10.

What is the definition of "selfless"? Being concerned with the needs and wishes of others rather than with personal concerns.

What is the definition of "worth"? The value equivalent to that of someone or something under consideration; the level at which someone or something deserves to be valued or rated.

What is selfless worth? Giving life to the value of others by inwardly searching to attribute significance, purpose, and meaning to someone other than oneself Many factors can lead to undermining relationships. However, two that stand out the most are arrogance and selfishness. In most relationships, both parties tend to think about themselves at one point or another. I was selfish until God showed me myself through another person being the same way and I found myself saying the same things the person would say to me. Now I see that the focus should not be on what someone does for us, but the person we need to appreciate.

Let's have a look at Luke 15:8-10 (NIV), "The parable of the lost coin." [8] *"Or suppose a woman has ten silver coins[a] and loses one. Doesn't she light a lamp, sweep the house and search carefully until she finds it?* [9] *And when she finds it, she calls her friends and neighbors together and says, 'Rejoice with me;*

I have found my lost coin.' ¹⁰ In the same way, I tell you, there is rejoicing in the presence of the angels of God over one sinner who repents."

We all have heard the saying, "You don't know what you have until it's gone." But in this case, the woman valued the coin before it was lost. In relationships, you have to ask yourself, "Do I value the person I am with?" I'm sure you are wondering why I used these Scriptures as an example when it comes to helping relationships. Sometimes we have to take the time to examine the worth of others.

CHAPTER 1

WHERE IS YOUR FOCUS?

PURPOSE   OR   PREFERENCE

Love enables us to see the good, but lust blinds us and disables our vision of the relationship. In a relationship, do you consider your own or the other person's interest? Is it purposeful or a preference? Let's look at it from this perspective. It's easy to overlook the penny and go for the quarter. Sometimes people get in preference mode basing their reason for wanting to date or have a relationship with someone by measuring their success, achievements, and social status within the community. Could there be an underlying motive? Yes, it could be, but not necessarily. It's okay to have a preference, but often good men and women have been overlooked due to not fitting the prototype. We can all have good intentions, but our intentions are undeniably guided by our preferences.

When dating for a preference, the intent is clear, but it seems that the focal point is set on expectations of the must haves, wants, maybes, and needs of both parties. However, it does not give value to the person or the relationship. During my teenage years, I dated a girl I thought was really interested in me but she was not genuine. After a week of talking, she avoided me in school and did not bother calling me. I asked a mutual friend of ours and the conversation went like this:

ME: *WHY HAS YOUR FRIEND STOP TALKING TO ME?*

FRIEND: *SHE SAID SHE DIDN'T LIKE THE TYPE OF CLOTHING YOU WEAR.*

ME: *WHAT'S WRONG WITH THE CLOTHES I WEAR?*

FRIEND: *SHE SAID YOU DON'T HAVE NO GEAR (TOP BRAND NAME CLOTHES).*

ME: *WELL, TELL HER I SAID BUY THE GEAR FOR ME THEN!!!!!!!*

As you can see from the conversation, it's obvious that her sense of fashion was more important than me. Now, this is not the case in all relationships or potential ones. When you date for a preference, you take for granted the importance of someone's time, life, and heart. When dating for a purpose, the intent is clear and goal-directed. It fulfills the desires of understanding each other, placement in each other's lives, but most importantly, the relationship's value is more appreciated.

Let's look at Matthew 9:10-13 (NIV).
[10] While Jesus was having dinner at Matthew's house, many tax collectors and sinners came and ate

with him and his disciples. ¹¹ When the Pharisees saw this, they asked his disciples, "Why does your teacher eat with tax collectors and sinners?"¹² On hearing this, Jesus said, "It is not the healthy who need a doctor, but the sick. ¹³ But go and learn what this means: 'I desire mercy, not sacrifice.'[a] For I have not come to call the righteous, but sinners."

As you can see from the Scriptures, Jesus' relationship building was not based on preference, but purpose. He valued the tax collectors and sinners too. Jesus showed the attitude that no one person is better than any person. Another way to look at it is you can have all the money, degrees, or accolades and still be treated as a nobody. What's important, the relationship or what the person owns? **JUST REMEMBER YOU ARE SOMEBODY!!!!!!!**

Be honest with yourself, which do you give more weight to concerning your relationship or potential relationship?

CHAPTER 2

SUPPORT SYSTEM

His battles. Her battles. His plans. Her plans. What about our battles? What about our plans?

One of the major key roles in a relationship is to be each other's support system. It's stressful enough dealing with circumstances that work against the relationship and each individual, but it can be more damaging when couples are working against each other.

Amos 3:3 says, "How can two walk together, except they be agreed."

The idea of building together requires negotiation or the art of compromise. It's not about giving up your career goals, dreams, and other plans. It is about making time to invest in each other, and growing as a team. The following are some questions you need to ask yourself when you get some quiet or downtime:

1. Am I trying to help better him/her?
2. What can I do to help enhance him/her?
3. What am I willing to sacrifice for the sake of building a future with this man/woman or bettering our relationship?
4. Why did I say yes to our relationship?

These are just a few questions to ponder because some goals may take people in different directions in either building relationships or becoming deal-breakers for them.

Take a moment to gather your thoughts. Reflect on the four questions above. Write down the goals for yourself and your spouse on the chart. What are your relationship goals?

Your Goals	Spouse/ Significant Other Goals

Relationship Goals

Another aspect to consider in this chapter is how will you react when oppression begins to attack the relationship? For example, let's consider ex-relationships. If children are involved, is there any mother and father drama? Is there a stained history that negatively stigmatizes the character of your partner? This can be a revealing factor to see if you will stand up for your relationship, or will you back away? Some people say they are with you, but they are unwilling to go through with you when the fire comes. These circumstances will reveal your level of commitment to each other.

Today many men and women have made a habit of breaking up their relationships, which has become a trend in this generation. Let's do an experiment and answer the following questions. Which of these couples are you and your partner at this very moment?

A (Couple above) I can't take this anymore. I'm fed up! We are done! It's over!!!!!!!!!!!!

Or

B (Couple above) We are going to get through this together.

If you chose A, what is your reasoning?

If you chose B, what is your reasoning?

After you have given your reasoning, discuss with your partner how you can improve to help the relationship grow. Afterward, refer back to question 4. Why did I say yes to our relationship? Now check out this YouTube video titled (Stop Saying I love you)

https://www.youtube.com/watch?v=mzd524x_2-I

Personal Notes

_____

_____

_____

_____

CHAPTER 3

MATTERS OF THE HEART

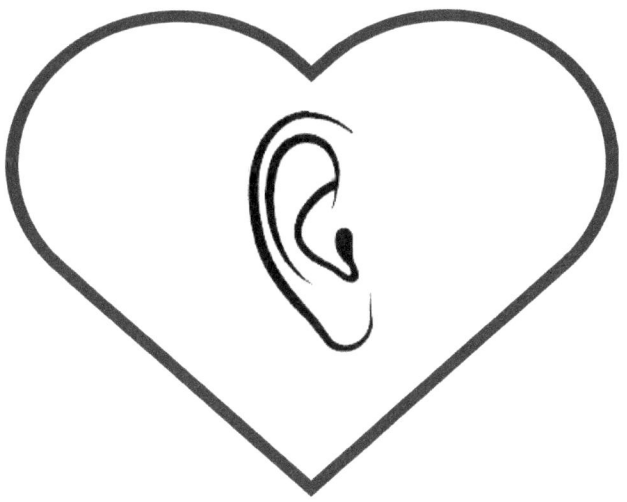

QUESTION: Who has your ear?

This is a rhetorical question. However, ponder this question and be honest.

Brace yourself for IMPACT! Wait! What does this mean? Well, let me put it to you like this. In this chapter, I want to breakdown and shed some light on two of the common denominators of relationship and marriage breakers, which are INFLUENCE and SABOTAGE. Sometimes it's the combination of them both.

What is influence? According to Merriam Webster, **it is the power or capacity to affect indirectly or in intangible ways**. It also means to sway. Some relationships have ended because of insiders on the outside, meaning other voices control and manipulate the flow of how you operate within your relationship. It results from communication with others about what's going on in the relationship or marriage, whether good or bad. Now to be clear, influences are not based solely on what you hear from other people. It can also be what is seen that can influence your relationship or marriage, such as statistics, other people's experiences, cultural, family or religious traditions, and beliefs. Below is a diagram of four categories of influence.

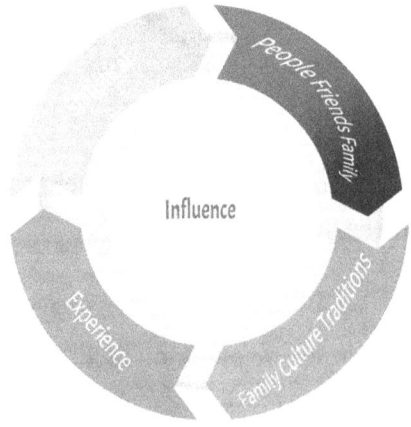

Influence	Description	Example	Effects of Influence
Statistical	Information or data that is comprised of percentages, ratios, rates, etc., to which the cause and effect of case by case basis of what happens.	There is a 45% rate of divorce that is happening in the church.	**Pros:** Maybe factual, but not 100% truth. **Cons:** Statistics can show an alarmingly high rate of negative information that can change your relationship perspective from positive to negative.

People, Friends & Family	People that know or don't you or your partner give information based on what they think they know: positive or negative.	The "he say" or "she say" chitter chatter.	**Pros:** Some people may give good advice on how to build a good relationship, what to watch out for and even help keep you in line about yourself. **Cons:** Close relatives and friends might be envious of what you have. They feel that because you all are close that if they

| | | | are in your ear, you will and should listen without consideration of the source. They don't know the truth about your mate or what goes on in your relationship. Everyone is not happy about your relationship. |

Family cultural, traditions, beliefs	Ideas, morals, and values that are taught in society from childhood to adulthood to follow as examples of standards in life.	The mother and or father have to like and approve their daughter's mate.	**Pros:** Some traditions and beliefs can help with checks and balances of having good principles and character: (morals). **Cons:** Set ways. There is no room for change or growth, which can cause one to not see or accept another aspect of life: (tunnel vision).

Experiences	Past relationship or incidents of your own or others. They can be even current, whether good or bad.	It's hard for me to trust someone to be in a relationship with because the last person cheated on me.	Pros: Gain wisdom, knowledge, maturity, and growth for how to handle yourself in future relationships. Cons: Bad experiences can cause you to have insecurities about being in a relationship or about your partner by comparing your current partner to your ex. Other people will base

			your relationship and issues on their bad experiences because of their own personal feelings.

Special Note – *Each category of influence has its own independent affect; However, each category can be affected by the other or act as a dependency upon each other, which can have more of an impact of influence.*

Is this you and your partner? Is it you? If so, how does this affect your relationship? If you are not in a relationship, how does it affect your expectations on the quest to find the person to date? Take the time to discuss amongst each other or reflect within yourself to see what impact it has made.

What is sabotage? According to the Merriam dictionary, sabotage **is to deliberately destroy, damage, or obstruct something**. Well, in this case, relationships and marriages. Understand that there are and will be people who are not fond of your relationship and will do anything to end it. Before you read more deeply into this part of the chapter, I would like for you to think about this familiar scenario. Do you remember Eve and the serpent in the Garden of Eden?

Genesis 3:1-6 says, "1Now the serpent was more subtil than any beast of the field which the Lord God had made. And he said unto the woman, Yea, hath God said, Ye shall not eat of every tree of the garden?2 And the woman said unto the serpent, We may eat of the fruit of the trees of the garden:3 But of the fruit of the tree which is in the midst of the garden, God hath said, Ye shall not eat of it, neither shall ye touch it, lest ye die.4 And the serpent said unto the woman, Ye shall not surely die:5 For God doth know that in the day ye eat thereof, then your eyes shall be opened, and ye shall be as gods, knowing good and evil.6 And when the woman saw that the tree was good for food, and that it was pleasant to the eyes, and a tree to be desired to make one wise, she took of the fruit thereof, and did eat, and gave also unto her husband with her; and he did eat."

Just think about it and hold your thoughts. You ask yourself, "Why would someone want to mess up my relationship and what I have hmmm? What did I do? Well, the answer to that is **NOTHING. THAT'S RIGHT ABSOLUTELY NOTHING !!!!!!!!!!** Some are jealous, envious, and insecure about what you have because they don't have it and or at one point, they probably did. Now, who would want to sabotage your relationship? Well, let's see ex-partners or **CLOSE RELATIVES!!!** Hold up. Wait a minute. Wait for it ………………….. oh, that's it; even people in the church. Oh wow! Don't be surprised if it's the ones called your friends. You can even sabotage your own relationship if you are looking for a reason to get out of it and the same goes for your current mate. It happens.

Be cautious of your circle. Be oblivious to who celebrates, when they celebrate, and how they celebrate you because it can be quite deceiving. Be careful of who you share personal information with, especially if you and your partner have a critical argument or disagreement because they can prey on the vulnerability with itching ears and seduce you with negative and disrupting ideas. Now here is the "Think Tank Moment." Notice above how close relatives and people in the church are emphasized. Now, answer the question: who wants to sabotage your relationship?

SELFLESS WORTH • 25

Earlier I asked you all to think about the scenario about Adam, Eve, and the Serpent as it pertains to relationships. Answer these questions.

1. What would you have done if you were in Adam's position and why?

2. What would you have done if you were in Eve's position and why?

3. Who did Adam blame for what happened?

CHAPTER 4

CONFLICT RESOLUTION

"CONFLICT NOT WAR"

Every relationship takes some work, whether it's construction or deconstruction. At some point, there will be a time when the relationship will have to face issues from within. It's a part of the relational building process. Sweeping things under the rug does not correct or fix the issue. You are just organizing a mess. You can't ignore it and hiding is useless. Conflict will happen in some shape or form. A couple needs to be able to come together to address the problem. I remember having a conversation with a good friend, Randy Ames. While talking, he said something that struck me in my thinking about relationships. He said, "Alex, it's not the lack of communication that causes the problems. However, it's the lack of honest communication." To love someone is to be truthful and not hide. At some point, some disagreements can lead to arguments, but how you handle the conflict is the question. Conflict can bring about growth, change and empowerment to a better working relationship **IF** handled the right way. Here are some things to consider when it comes to being truthful and honest.

- *Vulnerability* — Can you and your partner open up to each other?
- *Open-mindedness* — Can you see your partner's point of view?
- *Willingness to listen and give feedback*— Are you able to not dominate the conversation while hearing from your partner and then share your feelings?
- *Acceptance* — Are you willing to take what they are saying into consideration?
- *Rejection* — No one is willing to budge from their standpoint.

Here are some things that can cause conflict. However, these are the necessary conversations that need to happen at some point.

- *Correction* — Are you and your partner able to respectfully correct each other when someone does something wrong? Not pointing the finger, but truly understanding what went wrong?
- *Supportive goal ideas* — Do you have an open mind to receive ideas about your goals even if it means making a sacrifice from the original idea or not going with it?
- *Finances* — Who has better control of finances, budgeting, etc.?
- *Friendships of the opposite gender* — What are your feelings about your spouse's or partner's past and current relationships/friendships with the opposite sex?

These are just a few questions to ponder. Below are a few keys to help with damage control when disagreeing because fights can get ugly. This is not saying things can't get out of hand because not all arguments are the same.

1. Listen without interrupting.
2. Talk to and not at your mate.
3. You are not and don't have to always be right. Don't raise your tone of voice. Just raise the

tone of your argument. *Make a valid point without being harsh. It's not what you say. It's how you say it.*
4. **DO NOT INVOLVE OUTSIDE PEOPLE UNLESS IT'S A PASTOR OR RELATIONSHIP/MARRIAGE COUNSELOR!!!!!!!!!!**
5. **DO NOT LEAVE AN ARGUMENT OPEN with both of you angry at each other, not talking all day and night. Ephesians 4:26 (NIV) In your anger, do not sin.** <u>Do not let the sun go down while you are still angry.</u>
6. **DO NOT DO ANY BAD NAME CALLING AND REFRAIN FROM PROFANE LANGUAGE.**
7. THINK BEFORE YOU SPEAK!!!!!!!!!!! (Put yourself at the receiving end of a statement or comment. You want to make your partner see how it would affect you.)
8. THINK BEFORE YOU ACT!!!!!!! (Put yourself on the receiving end of the action you are pondering on doing to your partner.)

When we think about conflict or disagreements, we often look at them negatively simply because the outcomes aren't considered good. However, conflicts can bring about good change.

Take some time and ponder this: How has conflict affected your relationship/marriage? What changes do you and your mate see?

Positive Changes:

_____

_____

_____

_____

_____

_____

_____

Negative Changes:

_____

_____

_____

_____

_____

_____

_____

SELFLESS WORTH • 31

Proverbs 4:7 says, "Wisdom is the principal thing; Therefore, get wisdom: and with all thy getting get an understanding."

Being in a relationship or marriage can be challenging. However, they can be rewarding if you take the time to acknowledge the other person's value and worth. Give your partner assurance that their place in your life is purposeful and meaningful. It's one thing to take time to know one another, but another to take the time to build and grow with one another. So set a solid relationship foundation and LETS BUILD, SUSTAIN, AND MAINTAIN STRONG RELATIONSHIPS & MARRIAGES!!!!!!!!!!!!!!!!!!!!!!!!!!!!!!!!!!

The Greatest selfless act that ever took place.

John 3:16 says, "For God so loved the world, that he gave his only begotten Son, that whosoever believeth in him should not perish, but have everlasting life."

John 3:16 (NIV) says, "For God so loved the world that he gave his one and only Son, that whoever believes in him shall not perish but have eternal life."

***I want to challenge you. Do a self-evaluation on what you have invested in the relationship and your partner. Be truthful. Make a list of what you and your partner have done. Now here is where it gets challenging. Put yourself on the receiving end of what you have invested in the relationship and then assess, reevaluate, and determine what areas need to improve on your behalf while your partner does the same. One of the keys to a successful relationship is RECIPROCITY.

*NOTE: The effort put into the relationship shows your mindset, interest and maturity level.

BE HONEST WITH YOURSELF. DON'T BE AFRAID TO SEE YOURSELF IN THE AREAS YOU NEED TO BE BETTER!!!!!!!!!

Marriages, relationships, courtships are in critical condition and need urgent care. Divorce and breakup rates are on a high rise nationwide, even with leaders and church members. The following questions should be considered: What is happening? And WHY? Have we, as a society, neglected the reality of marriages or relationships? We have gotten into this mindset of individuality. Always wanting, but there's no reciprocity. So I urge and challenge you to do a self-evaluation. If you are in a marriage, relationship/courtship, or even looking to be involved with someone, ask yourself, "What am I willing to give for my spouse or partner to know that they are valuable to my life? (SELFLESS-WORTH)

Personal Notes:

_____

_____

_____

_____

_____

Personal Notes:

Personal Notes:

ABOUT THE AUTHOR

Alexander Young is an anointed man of God. He was born and raised on the Southside of Chicago, Illinois. He is a proud father of four boys and appreciative of having a strong supportive wife, Evelyn Whitfield Young, a woman of God and a minister of the Gospel. Mr. Young served 12 years in the United States Army, including three combat tours to Iraq. He was honorably discharged with the rank of Sergeant. Alexander has well deservedly earned numerous medals, badges, and awards during

his time of service. After the military, Elder Young went to further his education and obtained an Associate's degree in Human Resource Management and a Bachelor's in Business Management. Alexander does not take his calling lightly. He humbly accepts his role as a chosen vessel for the Kingdom.

Alexander Young received his calling to the ministry in July 2007 but did not walk in or accept his calling until December 2013. He has dealt with many obstacles and setbacks after his military service, but that did not stop him from accomplishing his goals. Before Alex became a minister at the church he currently attends, he served in different auxiliaries at a different church. He served as an usher for the church, in the choir, and also in the men's choir. While bouncing back from being homeless, Mr. Young has served within the community and became more successful, and achieved many accomplishments. He received a proclamation from the city Mayor. He is a co-author of a book titled "50 Magnificent Men" and also received his Ordination of Elevation from Minister to Elder. Not only does he serve in the capacity of a minister at his current church, but also he serves as the Bishop's Adjutant.

Alexander Young has a vision for the Kingdom and his purpose, which is for everyone to receive the Salvation and see the Glory of the Lord work in their lives. He has a passion to help the homeless and relationship building. Alexander walks in his purpose not to be like but because he is necessary and he will do whatever it takes to edify the Kingdom.

INDEX

A

accomplishments, 39
achievements, 5
acknowledge, 33
Adam, 27
Adjutant, 39
adulthood, 20
angels, 3
anger, 31
anointed, 38
appreciate, 2
appreciated, 6
AREAS, 34
argument, 26, 31
attack, 11
auxiliaries, 39
awards, 38

B

badges, 38
balances, 20
battles, 9
beliefs, 16, 20
budgeting, 30
building, 7, 9, 10, 28, 39

C

category, 24
celebrate, 26
cheated, 22
childhood, 20
church, 17, 26, 34, 39
circumstances, 9, 11
CLOTHING, 6
coin, 1, 2, 3
communication, 16, 29
community, 5, 39
concerns, 2
Conflict, 28, 29
Cons, 17, 18, 20, 22
conversation, 5, 6, 29
Correction, 30
COUNSELOR, 31
couples, 1, 9, 11
courtships, 34

D

damage, 24, 30
dating, 5, 6
degrees, 7
destroy, 24
disagreement, 26
disciples, 7
divorce, 1, 17
downtime, 10
drama, 11
dreams, 9

E

ear, 15, 19
edify, 39
education, 38
empowerment, 29
envious, 18, 26
Eve, 25, 27
evil, 25
expectations, 5, 24
experiment, 11

F

Family, 18, 20
fed up, 12

Finances, 30
flow, 16
focus, 2, 4
FRIEND, 6
Friends, 18
fruit, 25
future, 10, 22

G

Garden of Eden, 25
GEAR, 6
gender, 30
generation, 11
Glory, 39
goal-directed, 6
Goals, 10, 11
good, 4, 5, 16, 18, 20, 22, 25, 29, 31
growth, 20, 22, 29

H

habit, 11
happy, 19
harsh, 31
healthy, 7
heart, 6, 15
help, 10, 13, 18, 20, 30, 39
homeless, 39

honest, 7, 15, 29
house, 2, 6

I

ideas, 26, 30
IMPACT, 15
incidents, 22
INFLUENCE, 16
insecure, 26
insecurities, 22
invest, 9

J

jealous, 26
Jesus, 1, 6, 7

K

Kingdom, 38, 39
knowledge, 22

L

lamp, 2
leaders, 34
life, 1, 2, 6, 20, 33, 34, 35
light, 2, 15

listen, 19, 29
love, 13, 29
lust, 4

M

marriage breakers, 16
married, 1
mate, 19, 20, 26, 30, 32
maturity level, 34
medals, 38
military, 38, 39
mindset, 34, 35
ministry, 38
money, 7
morals, 20
motive, 5

N

needs, 2, 5, 28
negative, 17, 18, 26
negotiation, 9
nobody, 7
non-married, 1

O

obstacles, 39

Open-mindedness, 29
oppression, 11

P

Parable, 1
partner, 11, 13, 18, 22, 24, 26, 29, 30, 31, 33, 34, 35
passion, 39
PASTOR, 31
penny, 1, 4
percentages, 17
Pharisees, 7
placement, 6
plans, 9
position, 27
positive, 17, 18
preference, 4, 5, 6, 7
principles, 20
problem, 29
proclamation, 39
PROFANE LANGUAGE, 31
Pros, 17, 18, 20, 22
prototype, 5
purpose, 2, 6, 7, 39
PURPOSE, 4

Q

quarter, 4
question, 13, 15, 26, 29
questions, 10, 11, 27, 30, 34

R

Randy Ames, 29
rates, 17, 34
ratios, 17
reasoning, 13
reciprocity, 35
reevaluate, 34
Rejection, 29
Rejoice, 2
relationships, 1, 2, 3, 6, 10, 11, 16, 22, 27, 29, 30, 34, 35
relatives, 18, 26
religious traditions, 16
repents, 3
righteous, 7
roles, 9

S

SABOTAGE, 16
sacrifice, 7, 10, 30
Salvation, 39
scenario, 25, 27
Scriptures, 3, 7

self-evaluation, 34, 35
selfish, 1, 2
selfless, 2, 33
serpent, 25
service, 38, 39
setbacks, 39
sex, 30
silver, 2
sinner, 3
social status, 5
society, 20, 35
Son, 33, 34
source, 19
SPEAK, 31
standpoint, 29
Statistical, 17
stressful, 9
success, 5
sun, 31
SUPPORT, 9
Supportive, 30

T

tax collectors, 6, 7
Think Tank Moment, 26
truth, 17, 19
truthful, 29, 34

U

ugly, 30
understanding, 6, 30, 33

V

value, 1, 2, 3, 5, 6, 33
vision, 4, 20, 39
voice, 30
vulnerability, 26

W

wants, 5, 26
WAR, 28
WEAR, 6
wisdom, 22, 33
wishes, 2
worth, 1, 2, 3, 33

Y

YouTube, 13

www.ingramcontent.com/pod-product-compliance
Lightning Source LLC
LaVergne TN
LVHW020437080526
838202LV00055B/5236